Events and Beginnings

A Collection of Odds and Ends

Thirty-three and one third (33$\frac{1}{3}$) Poems

by

Remo Perini

Perini, Remo.
Evens and Beginnings,
A Collection of Odds and Ends.
[1. Poetry]

ISBN: 979-8-9858877-6-1 (hardcover)
ISBN: 979-8-9858877-7-8 (soft cover)

Table of Contents

Table of Contents

DEDICATION

This work is dedicated to my mother, Elizabeth (Betsy) Catherine Holden Perini. My mother introduced me to cream cheese and date-nut bread, peas, carrots, and potatoes, black pudding, pasta, and corporal punishment. She is a loving mother that stood by her children during difficult times, such as being bullied at school, physical injuries, and emotional distress. The strength of her love made her children what they are today. She taught us to be thoughtful, introspective people that define themselves through integrity and generosity, with an added dose of curiosity and wonder.

My mother's upbringing included the Great Depression and a Scottish household with lots of potatoes. As a child her family had little to offer her, but as an adult, she got both a Bachelor's and a Master's degree to better provide for her family. She was the elementary school's art teacher and we had a large art studio attached to our house. She welded, spun and kiln-dried pottery, sculpted dancers, mandalas, and family members' heads.

She had an electrolysis business on the side to make extra money. Mom hosted all of our elementary school parties in our backyard.

She learned to scuba dive to please my father and even moved to Key Largo for twenty-something years following his dreams. Her dreams were the successes of her children: a medical doctor, a home builder, a successful stock-market investor, a business owner, a restaurant owner, a sailor, a real estate mogul, a musician, and a writer. These attributes are those of her two sons of which I am the eldest and least successful (please buy this book).

She is a beautiful person who has continually made suggestions on how to improve this book, asking important question such as, "Who would want to read this?" and "Why would anybody buy it?"

Betsy currently lives in Scottsdale AZ, near her more well-endowed son, my younger and considerably more financially successful brother, Sean. Though mom has been blind for many years due to macular degeneration, she frequently states that she needs to get a car so she can be more active. As this dedication is written, Mom is nearing 90, living in her own home, with daily elder care support to help her with such things as: everything. We speak every day and she is quick to laugh at a joke, but still insists on giving advice on even the most esoteric topics, such as neurocognitive response research, and iambic pentameter. I hope she will like this book.

FOREWORD

The writing of this book spans decades; through lonely times, times of profound love and affection, sad times, and times of great joy. Some of these emotions are well represented here, as are some times of silliness. I think we can all see ourselves in these pages, and perhaps see others in them as well

The bits and pieces of Remo that fill these pages are haphazardly strewn and do not tell a carefully woven tale or paint a discernable picture. I will offer you this: I love words, and love to mold not only the phrases and thoughts they combine to build, but mold the words themselves. Mixing a Latin prefix with a Greek root and a slang suffix can be fun as long as the meaning can be understood. Kurt Vonnegut was a master; I am a neo-proto-padawan.

I must admit that I am not a student of poetry and do not actively consider meter or structure. I write to express feelings. At times, I may feel like writing but do not have a subject, so I start writing words and sentences or stanzas that sound good to my ear. And if I chance upon a verse or a rhyme or a pretty phrase, I may build upon that and revise the antecedent material to support the piece of beauty I have stumbled across.

The art that accompanies my words is either by Frankie McCarthy, a Vienna Virginia local artist, or free downloadable art from the wonderful photographers at Pexels.com. The reference to 33 1/3 poems is a nod to my many years as a radio station on-air DJ, spinning, 33 1/3" vinyl records. As a self-anointed literary artist, I reserve the right to label the short version of *Til Death Do Us Part* as the one third, hence 33 1/3 poems.

Not all the work included in this tome is beautiful. Some is harsh, some is simple, and some may be sad. But so is life. Like a Japanese garden that purposely builds in a defect, this work is strewn with imperfections that like a beloved teddy bear has a thrice-sewn ear, a worn-out nose, and stitching apparent throughout. But it is your bear or your child's bear, or the bear of a stranger's child you see in the mall, and as you look upon it, you recognize that it symbolizes innocence and love, and it makes us smile, perhaps because we miss that innocence, or perhaps we don't know why we smile, but we do.

May the bits and pieces of you blend well with the bits and pieces of me in this book, and it is my hope you will find a smile, some joy, some memories and some curiosity to sustain your journey through these pages

A creation. Laid out, dark and foreboding.
A mark; placed within emptiness.
No longer empty, barren or pure.... there exists.
Something to be investigated, something to learn.
A creation with form. Perceived, radiant and compelling.

A thought; meaning where once was none.
An entity, graspable, tenable and identifiable... a symbol.
Something to question, something that may be understood.
A creation that endures.

Existing and relinquishing existence.
A word, laid gently to rest.
To be communicated, translated and passed on... forever.
Something permanent, something that defines its own reality.

This is.

THE PROFIT PROPHET

The profit prophet comes to town and snickers at his host.
Our money, gold, and ivory, are what we cherish most.
He prophesies a number, and sells it with a grin,
We sell our souls, our happiness and let the wheels spin.

We trust his premonition; it hasn't failed us yet.
And when the jackpot has been won, we gladly pay our debt.
We pay from deep within ourselves, our spirits and our drives,
He takes our warmth, our tenderness,
The meanings of our lives.

We're trading our humanity for riches, wealth, and gold,
The profit prophet gets his fee, the happiness we've sold.
For just a smile he'll call a score and frowning we will win,
Our smiles are gone, the coins we've gained,
Have turned our hearts to tin.

We've always wanted riches, no matter what the cost,
But now that we possess them, we wonder what we've lost.
Perhaps one day we'll realize, a vision from above,
The profit prophet brought us wealth,
But now we don't have love.

TOMORROW'S YESTERDAY

Tomorrow's Yesterday is winding down... again,
With everything to show for it in a pointed gesture.
Sometime and somewhere feel for a forever onward tailspin,
With *Never* among the luxuries to console.

Dreams fondle our reality with glimpses of fleeting fantasy.
Rivers of opportunity unfold before us,
Options left behind evaporate with every step.
Atop a near hill lies a two-car garage.
A large fallow field offers an enormous rosewood desk.
Around and up is wealth beyond compare,
Guarded by the angry toll of loneliness.
And along another road espousal waits,
With joy and love and companionship.

Each path is paved with possibilities,
Cobbled with countless opportunities.

Some are certain, some unsure and some are clearly laid.
For those who have auspicious goals, the preacher must be paid.

But daring not to take a step and waiting for a clue,
Will cause each day to wind on down,
With nothing shed anew.
So cast your caution to the wind,
With courage take a chance.
You'll find your dream, your wealth, your quest,
A beautiful romance.

Embark upon a voyage, for movement is the key,
The essence of a future dream, a new reality.
Before Tomorrow's Yesterday has made its final bow,
Release your fear and take one step,
No better time than now.

3

CANDLELIGHT

Candlelight in a dark, dark room,
Canvas white in the starkness.
A dream awaits, glowing in the bare surroundings...
And the Canvas calls to it.

A brush, a gentle stroke, a splash of color,
Capturing an image, a patterned poem, a painted phrase.
Darkness recedes with each brushed caress and the
starkness is Dreamlit.
The Canvas is vibrant, luminous, incandescent.

The room no longer dark,
By the light of a single candle.

THE KING

A dark blue cloak thrown back by a damp chill wind.
In the cold fading light appears a sullen figure in soiled garments.
Another pace and the air is thick with his horse's musty breath.
He dismounts his tired steed, and approaches, head held high.
To pass these walls he must be friend, not foe.

His countenance looms larger than his stature.
He offers an outstretched hand.
His touch reveals overwhelming tenderness.
In the waning light his gaze is bright with a gleam in his eye,
A smile beneath his beard.
His presence offers sudden warmth, and the feel of strength,
and power and magnificence.
It is he! It is he! Our King has returned!

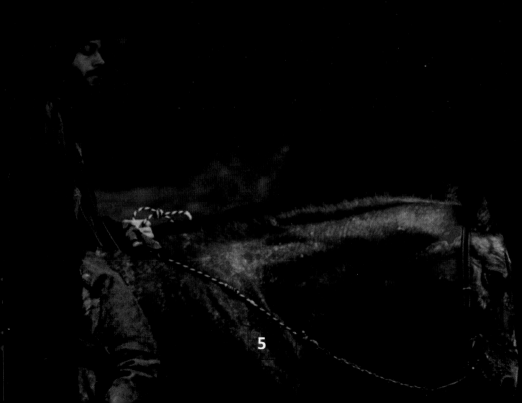

TANGLE ARE WE

Material strengthens with hardness the abstract.
The scholar bends his trade.
No descriptions are necessary,
No prizes for profound conjecture.
Things touching things called this or that,
Catalogue and sample, shape, and color,
Size and name.
Theory lends no construction of why or how,
Demanding an effort to explain.

Tangle are we that remain of thought,
Complexious, Chaoticism, Confucius,
Reluctantly, I reach to grasp your reality,
Your models, your behavior.
With a loving embrace, you remodel my originality.
As I accede to conform, my light darkens.
And with the wings of time,
You disappear me.

NEW THOUGHT

Searching inwardly through
the Farthest reaches of
consciousness,
I find a colorless presence,
hiding in an unused corner,
shielding itself from my
silent inward probing.

Touching upon it,
I realize it is a new thought,
An awareness not
previously considered,
A small speck of wonder that has
been hidden throughout my entire
life. Gently I embrace this thought,
Slowly I caress its meaning.
As I invitingly attempt to bring
it out of the corner, into the
forefront of my consciousness,
it begins to dissipate,
warning me of its sensitivity
and fragility. I back off,
and tracing my path
so that I may return,
take another sip of
coffee, and turn the
page of my notebook.

SECLUSION

Seen from afar,
A memory becomes unbalanced.
A depth of stillness, rising in vain,
Told of misery, heartache and pain.
Another figment; solitude and a desert.
The dance of one bear in a cave all alone.

Hearting toward seclusion folds,
Nowhere becomes adrift too soon.
Taken then, ashore by your vision,
To another turn, another road,
Another song.

NOBODY

Leaky faucet, dirty sheets and a forty-watt light bulb.
Eleventh floor single bedroom
with a view of the cemetery
beyond the roof of a supermarket.
No telephone in the apartment.
Nothing to say.
Nobody to say it to.
Welfare check comes tomorrow.

Disheveled closet, polo gear on the floor,
And an overcrowded bookcase.
Summer home on the lake,
And the clay tennis court needs to be swept.
A revolver lies on the floor.
Next to it a broken man,
Who had nothing to look forward to.
Nobody to share it with.
Nobody to say it to.

OCEAN AND THE COASTAL LANDS

Crashing onto hot white sand, a salty wave appears,
To seek the warm sands of the beach,
Then dribble back like tears.
The tidal forces of romance had drawn my heart to yours,
And I, a swelling ocean wave, came dancing to your shores.

Approaching with a mighty surge, impassioned salty spray,
But then retreating with the wind, your love was kept at bay,
With every wave that reaches shore, a spurt of ecstasy,
Embracing sun warmed sandy dunes, my coastal destiny.

Every time the tide rolls in, I seek to win your heart,
You stroke my soul on golden sands, but with each tide I part.
The seaweed and the foamy surf dry up upon the shore,
Waves recede to gather strength, returning with a roar.

Our love will ebb and surge at times, but every seventh wave,
Will bring the softness of your smile, the tenderness I crave.
The surf sound sings a siren song, a whispered harmony,
That tells of white sand beaches, reaching for the sea.

One day we found beneath the waves, a treasure chest of love,
From watery depths we worked as one to bring it up above.
The chest we'd found was barnacled, encrusted, damp and old,
But when the padlocks were removed,
Its contents were pure gold.

The ocean and the coastal lands were lovers from that day,
Embracing one another, at capes and coves and quays.
You reach toward my horizon, and I reach to your shore,
The beach is where our hearts have found,
A love forever more.

OUR COUNTRY 'TIS

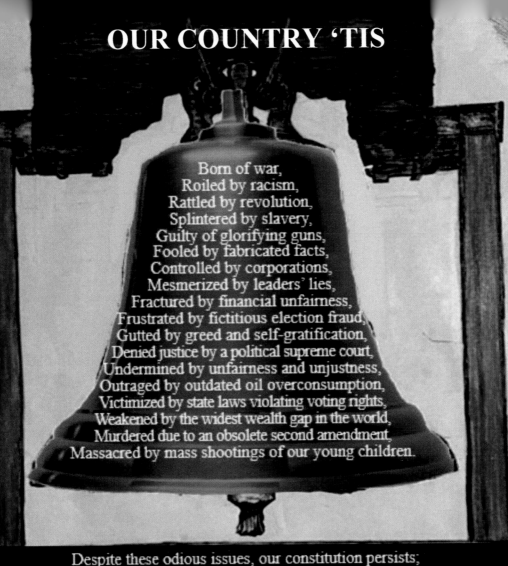

Born of war,
Roiled by racism,
Rattled by revolution,
Splintered by slavery,
Guilty of glorifying guns,
Fooled by fabricated facts,
Controlled by corporations,
Mesmerized by leaders' lies,
Fractured by financial unfairness,
Frustrated by fictitious election fraud,
Gutted by greed and self-gratification,
Denied justice by a political supreme court,
Undermined by unfairness and unjustness,
Outraged by outdated oil overconsumption,
Victimized by state laws violating voting rights,
Weakened by the widest wealth gap in the world,
Murdered due to an obsolete second amendment,
Massacred by mass shootings of our young children.

Despite these odious issues, our constitution persists;
We survived a mass insurrection,
Led by anger and white knuckled fists.
It's tremendously clear that we don't think as one,
So, let's start where we agree. We can find worthy
ways to accelerate growth, with a path for all to succeed.
Let's strengthen our great intuitions, 'til the anger and fury
has quelled. It's time to "chillax" and debate with respect,
With ethical conduct upheld.
Let's look past the hate, and build on what's great,
We can overcome all the invective.
Freedom, and Liberty, and Justice for All,
Is still the world's greatest objective.

'TIL DEATH
DO US PART

To offer one's life to another,
And promise 'till death do us part,
Is a sentiment held, hoping two lives will meld,
Sharing feelings that come from the heart.
But questions emerge if the two lives diverge,
As to whom was the promise intended,
Should the vow that was granted, be sadly recanted,
For the terms of that promise have ended.

The friendship has waned,
and tensions have strained,
And passion is greatly diminished.
You barely are able to talk at the table,
And leave before dinner is finished.
You no longer like going on a long hike,
Or the fun things you once did together,
Like watching a show, with a glass of Bordeaux,
And playing at home in bad weather.

So, who is this person that's made your life worse in
The short time that you've been united?
You argue and shout and you never go out,
How could you have been so short sighted.
They don't say good night, like an unending fight,
Sometimes they don't even come home,
You sleep separated, touch re-pudiated,
You may as well live life alone.

(Continued)

'TIL DEATH
DO US PART
(Continued)

From your recollection,
There were <u>no</u> imperfections.
Their flaws had been totally hidden,
They don't show much shame,
For what they became.
Their hostility came quite unbidden.
Birthday's forgotten are especially rotten;
You spend special nights with a friend.
Your heart's been neglected. No longer respected,
You just want the heartache to end.

Lest there still be confusion,
True love's an illusion,
And searches for soul mates misguided.
If the soul does exist,
Then so far, it's been missed,
By the research that science provided.
For two lives to merge,
You must strive to converge,
Toward goals that you both can aspire.
The search for perfection can lead to rejection,
So, seek only traits you require.

And so, one should think before signing in ink,
To devote your whole life to a mate,
That in just a short time, for no reason or rhyme,
Love sometimes can turn into hate.
Live under one roof and gather the proof
You can both weather storms without strife,
Don't give an oath, 'til together you've both,
Shared the best and the worst things in life.

'Til Death DO US Part

(Short Version)

You said and I said,
'Till death do us part,
But you're not the same person,
I promised my heart.

The death that we spoke of,
Has killed our affection,
With sadness and fighting,
With pain and rejection.

I no longer see,
The one I first kissed,
The "you" that I loved,
Has now ceased to exist.

No need for good-byes,
Or pretended affections,
Without handshake or hug,
We'll go separate directions.

WE ARE TWO I'S

Tarnished planking. Barnacled grapes.
The tenth of every breath.
Challenge the fever,
Its stake is not our spoils.
Harlequin harlots, Transient talcum.
Wherefore the cellar door?
Beseeching rivalry,
No plan survives Spartan toils.
We are rushing, yes and you.
Erstwhile jewels of future friends.
Stringent softness now oblique,
Taken ashore by wanton chance.
Strangle and struggle
in the shadowed street.
Strange you did not hear?
I am near, you are far.
Heretofore, the poets dance.
We are two I's, this me and you.
Seek to blend, spurn to bend.
Acquiescent reticence trials forevermore,
Despite cherishing the essence.
The next is yet, but yet is still further.
Peering. Squinting. Blind.
Challenged by the wings of time,
Our sullied souls still
Search for semblance.

SEAFARER'S MANTLE

I hasten afore thy spirit turns restless
and thy quill is jettisoned.
Lest the passion grow fleeting and our marrow halved.
Damnable duty that doth betray passions depth.

Having met the enemy: the hours grew to
days and became weeks.
As the calendar savaged my countenance,
Distance disquieted my vision.
Reverently returning, the adversaries of time and
Distance mostly vanquished, Peering beyond the yardarms,

Amidst this yeoman's cry, desirous yearnings aspire welcome embrace.
Forward of the mizzen since early light, the mist hides green, not blue,
Anticipation and impatience become adrift,
With anxious moments mounting blindly.

A hopeful climb to perching nest, seeking promontory,
Rainful wind slaps audacious brow,
Seeking glimmers through drizzled haze,
Between stinging pelts and harrowed hail,
Glimpse of green and hints of hills,
Reveals the longed-for coast and thoroughfare,
And beyond a hill, a house, a heart.
Crying with the wind, uncertain what landfall will afford.

In hopes that heart is yearning mine, this seafarer's mantle doth rejoin.
In port, the distance now but minutes, no promise is assured, no omen is
foretold. The sails dropped, the ship is berthed, upon the dock a visage spied.
In frock and hood, upon the harbor dock, it could, it might, perhaps it is.

With pounding heart, descending to the pier, through jostling crowds,
A few more steps as the clouds above suddenly open,
Spilling sunlight on a frock of silk, the hood thrown back to reveal
Curls of crimson locks, open arms, and a squeal of joy.
A broad smile cracks my cheeks, my tears are loosed,
And life begins anew.

THE FROGS

The Frogs are coming.
In countless numbers they are hopping toward us.
Like a giant green warted wave they approach,
Too many to control, croaking as they come.
We stare in disbelief.
What do they want? Where did they come from?
Soon we will know, but how will all it end?
They may want retribution
For their legs that we have eaten.
Suddenly a large swarm of flies' buzzes by,
Toward the tide of frogs, and beyond.
And with the passage of flies, so too go the Frogs.
They are hopping away now,
Perhaps to get the flies.
Everything is calm.

SECRET

Thankful posture in the breeze on the sand
And a seabird squawks the secret.
Jet black twilight in the morning on the hill,
Finishing a thought with an ear to the sky.
Stagger through a mad dance,
In the lane all surround;
Having heard your whisper on the shore,
And on the hill,
My lips are sealed.

THE PULSE OF PEACE

Skipping lazily through partial harmonics,
A tune is tasted, tingling time.
To an open ear, a taste of brightness,
An absolute abounding rhyme.
Weaving, wandering, welcome sound,
Soothes and slides while shifting round.
Sweet and sour, a tempoed ode,
Brass are blaring, strings are bowed.

Incantations harmonied,
Rhythmic background, melodic lead.
Dancing wildly, on our feet,
The tunes enchant the city street.
Within the sound of center stage,
Laughs and smiles of every age.
With heartfelt glee, the crowd's elation,
We whistle praise, applause, ovation.

You can't love music and harbor hate, for music's charm should mitigate,
The anger, spite, hostility, replacing hate with chivalry.
Could spreading rhyme help decrease crime?
Trade politics for drummer's sticks?
For those that find their music sacred, can it be used to conquer hatred?

The joy of music renders gladness.
It can even quash, gut-wrenching sadness.
Can we expand its application,
To prevent war in every nation?
For hunger, greed, and crime to cease,
Let music bring a welcomed peace,
We cannot fight while humming tunes,
Lay down the guns, give up the dunes.

It seems far-fetched, for music to star,
In building brotherhood, ending war.
But if our planet's rocking out,
A wave of love may soon breakout,
While music cannot feed the poor,
It'll stir the rich, to give much more,
As music's beats are amplified,
The pulse of peace is heard world-wide.

DAYDREAM

I cannot sleep with my mind wandering about.
I try to rest on a single thought, but it too causes doubt and anxiety.

My daydreams are confusing and trying at their best.
I wish that I could just relax and get some needed rest.
I'm propped up on one elbow, a ballpoint in my hand,
I write some thoughts and lay back down and think of other lands.

A fairy tale princess is riding on the beach,
With auburn hair and fancy robes, she's just beyond my reach.
She looks to see me running and stops her strong white steed,
And as I reach to touch her, her shoulder starts to bleed.
A soldier stands with smoking gun atop an army tank.
The captain shouts an order, they plan to rob a bank.
The tellers are excited, they quickly count their cash,
And placing it in jelly jars, consolidate the stash.
The painters splash in frenzied haste to capture this strange scene.
No cameras are permitted, by orders of the queen.
The army tank is milking cows, the princess jumping rope,
The group of weary soldiers have given up all hope.

I don't remember anymore, my thoughts no longer filled.
Relaxing sleep is on the verge, my ballpoint has been stilled.

OUR SONG

Our song had been growing toward
A grand crescendo for 90 bars,
When suddenly this weekend,
The brass stopped blaring,
The timpani stilled and the violins
played a disconcerting refrain,
In a troubling minor key,
Bereft of saxophone.
The shift in tempo was so ominous
That even the conductor
lost his balance.

I'll never forget
How the woodwinds saved the day.
First the clarinets tentatively
Suggested a brief respite,
Gingerly advancing a reminder
Of the beautiful theme
That had been interrupted.
The flutes joined in,
Quietly resuming the major key,
We are now entering
The 93rd bar of our song,
And the melody has resumed,
Even more powerful than before.
Just when we thought
The crescendo had reached a climax,
The brief refrain has shown us
That the first movement,
Has only just begun.

CALAMITY AND CHAOS

Calamity and chaos, are hampering our lives,
We're stressed out due to jobs and bills and traffic on our drives.
We're frustrated at home because of busy hectic days,
And when we're home together, our patience runs astray.

Let's look upon the ocean, for learned sage advice,
The ocean can be turbulent, or peaceful, calm and nice,
But even when its stormy, with whitecaps, surf, and swells,
There is a place that's placid, where tranquility still dwells.

Down below the surface, its calm, cool, and serene,
Unlike the stormy shallows where chaos reigns supreme.
And like the deep blue ocean, we too can find some peace,
By looking passed the surface to our spirits underneath.

We need to look far deeper than the daily irritation,
Beyond our jobs, the house, the lawn,
And all the aggravation.
We've heard it said that Love can be
A powerful emotion,
Let's use our Love to get beyond
The surface of our Ocean.

The turbulence that wracks our lives,
and makes our days unpleasant,
Should be a shadow of our past,
and vanquished from our present.
The things that cause our rash disputes,
Are really not extensive,
To overcome these irritants,
Would make life less oppressive.

Our Love can be a diving bell, that helps relive our stress,
To take us past the shallowness and help to reassess.
The current at the surface, the blowing wind, and rain,
Is like the traffic on the road, an overcrowded train.

So, when we're feeling angry, or frustrated, or sore,
Let's contemplate the ocean, just beyond the shore.
Let's get below the surface of the anger, stress, and strife,
And find a place where we can be,
A joyful man and wife.

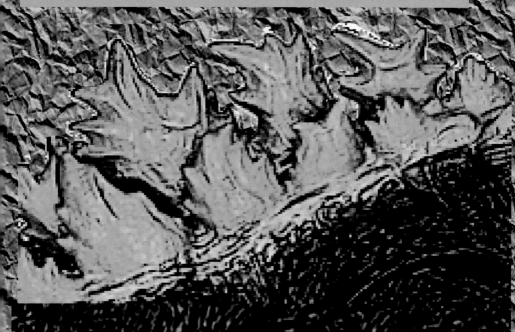

GODZILLA MISUNDERSTOOD

Gift or curse?

Overcoming self-image issues at a young age.

Defined to be known for fierce fiery breath.

Zigzagging through a tortuous life.

I find myself with arms too short to embrace

Love of any kind.

Looking for happiness and searching for

A place where I can live in peace.

ANGER RERLINQUISHED

My anger is relinquished with my pen.
The thought that these words may be read,
And then tossed away,
Reminds me that I can share my pain with others,
And they will help me to dispose of it.

CHILDREN'S DREAMS

Forget the wandering if the palace is near.
Continue the search should the feeling pale.
Embracing a light that warms the tide,
An angel opens the door to crystal prophecies,
A garden of ecstasy and a realm
of children's dreams.

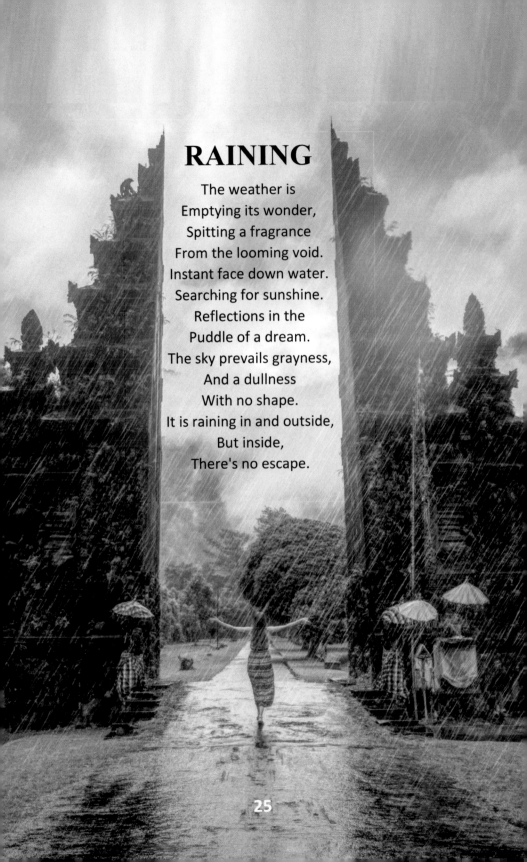

RAINING

The weather is
Emptying its wonder,
Spitting a fragrance
From the looming void.
Instant face down water.
Searching for sunshine.
Reflections in the
Puddle of a dream.
The sky prevails grayness,
And a dullness
With no shape.
It is raining in and outside,
But inside,
There's no escape.

FRIGHTMARE

Darkling tonight, illusive quiet pain.
Sharpening the images, a desert in the rain,
Sandwiched with a rose and a time and a thought.
Dancing far too freely, my dreams become distraught.

Awaiting tranquil dawn, implored eradication,
Thoughts of sunrise gentle light, a whispered incantation,
First glimmer yields a promise, a fragile, tempered bloom.
Dispels the fearsome frightmare, as shadows leave the room.

THE EYES OF THE GODDESS

All of us are equal in the eyes of the Goddess.
We venerate her wisdom, but we do not have her eyes,
We see things as imperfect, finding faults that we despise,
Not learning from the consequence, that teach it is unwise,
We're trapped with all our biases; at best we compromise.

MIRROR

You do not need a mirror,
To see things in reverse.
We hang with those that think like us,
Which makes the matter worse.

We need un-slanted media,
That's clear and plainly sourced.
Where news is never partisan,
No party is endorsed.

We need to calm the rhetoric,
Respect each other's views.
And jointly seek the middle ground,
With neutral honest news.

We need to understand the facts,
That fostered our perspective,
Because, without clear evidence,
Our argument's defective.

We're so convinced of our beliefs,
No matter how perverse,
By seeking facts, we all might find,
The truth is the reverse.

27

ALTITUDE ABOVE

Looking down from high above,
Life seems to pass so swift.
Like dreams contained in looking glass,
In miniature adrift.
Our destiny, our landing field,
Awaits our sleepful heads,
If outbound to an office.
If returning to our beds.

Soaring high above the clouds,
We seem to master time,
But can't control our destiny
Or hasten the sublime.
The ETA we've scheduled,
Will sometimes come in late,
And like the Airport of our lives,
We cannot predict fate.

MONARCH OF THE FIELDS

I've tried to be poetic and paint some thoughts of you.
Our friendship shows ambition, with sadness peeking through.
I see a pretty maiden, who calls this world her own,
But seeks for what she most desires, a love she's never known.

Your realm: idyllic prairie, as far as eyes can see,
Your passion is a golden field, that flows on endlessly.
With manners, class and elegance, a smile within your eyes,
But kept contained in castle walls, a wetness fills your skies.

Your chin held high with self-respect, an Aire of dignity,
A dangling strand of long brown hair like wheat blown by the breeze.
The sun has warmed your radiance, your harvest has come due,
To reap your love a noble man of greatness to pursue.

Pride tempered by innocence, your partner must be strong,
With delicate affection, your heart might still be won.
Your challenging endeavor: one worthy of your love.
A gentle breeze to take your life, enfold it like a glove.

As sunlight fades into the West in royal purple hues,
At rainbow's end a prince may wait, but is it you he'll choose?
Seek not the station of your mate, seek one that makes life fun.
With passion to cure loneliness, and sadness to expunge.

For having class and affluence is not the highest goal,
One's glamor might be artwork, that covers up a hole.
Be not afraid to show your love, your feelings, heart, and mind,
I know you'll find a gentleman who's loving, sweet, and kind.

STRUMMING ON
THE OLD BANJO

At the end, the very end,
I ponder and self-reflect.
What did I accomplish?
Not much that anyone
will care about when I am gone.
Did I bring joy to others? I think so.
Will I be leaving this place better
than when I arrived?
If so, only in a very small way.
Did I touch the world in a meaningful way?
And live a life of lasting value? Not really.

At this moment there is sadness in those
around me because I am leaving.
Leaving a space where I once stood,
Where I once smiled,
Where I once loved, and laughed, and cried.
I no longer have the power to turn sadness into joy,
But I did, and the younger person that took pride
In bringing happiness to others is deep within me now,
Still looking out, but helpless to act as I once did.

I used to worry whether my children would be OK. They will
be. I used to worry about leaving problems
behind for others to fix; I do not think I have.
There is no more worry, no more plans,
no more future, just right now.
Regrets? Certainly nothing of great consequence,
And it is quite too late to care even if there were.
I may have worried too much about such things,
but learning to shed that burden is A lesson learned far too late.

As a man I cherished humor, food, writing, and music.
My food now comes through an intravenous tube,
I can no longer conjure a laugh. And these are my last words,
penned when I still could type.
So, I am left with music, which is a nice ending.

(continued)

30

STRUMMING ON
THE OLD BANJO
(Continued)

I have a selfish request, but request it I will:
I ask those of you that I leave behind to whom I was close,
Think of me when you are enjoying a beautiful melody,
An outstanding performance,
or a song that perhaps we once shared.
I could say that I will be listening along with you,
But I really do not know if that is possible.
The scientist in me says it is not.
But we can hope that some form of us persists
After our bodies stop working.
And if so, I hope to watch you in your happiness,
And perhaps protect you in some manner during difficult times.
It's a nice thought and it brings joy and peace to
think this may be true.
So, let's just leave it at that.

I leave with joyful memories of a full
life that ends as they all do,
But without fear and with pride for the wonderful children,
To whom I pass the baton.
That is now all I have to give.
It is not enough, but it is all that is left in me.
I wish I had given more when I could.

I wanted to keep this ending sweet and upbeat.
You know how much I love you, and I know you love me.
So, in these last moments I have one more musical request:
Crank up the music and dance by my bedside.
Sing out loud and sing off key.
My heart will be dancing and singing along with you,
Strumming on the Old Banjo.

AWAKENING

Awakened on the steps of transcendent reality,
Grasping to reach the next plateau of sensibility.
Searching for purpose within space and time,
Layers of awareness and perception must be climbed.
Innumerable realities surround infinite dreams,
Some awkwardly bounding prohibitive schemes.
Benevolence censures a scripture that binds,
Encouraging curious, questioning minds.

Peeling away at a drab, thread-worn skin,
Astonishing freedom prevails within.
Discard liturgy, scripture, faith, and compliance,
To find beautiful rapture in spiritual science.
To embrace this connection is a meaningful step,
Now look deep within where your spirit is kept.
Extinguishing ego, desire and fear,
There's a place beyond Silence
When your mind has been cleared.

With this new insight, you should now realize,
You are linked to a Cosmos of infinite size.
With each nimble step, that connection increases,
To a greater awareness and the selflessness, it teaches.
The road to Nirvana is only a guide,
Subsequent footholds are found only inside.
The path to Enlightenment can answer life's call,
Epiphany and Illumination yield Oneness with all.

To shed all discernment, all concepts, all thoughts,
Is the path to Awakening which cannot be taught.
Unburden your senses and empty your mind....

AFTERWORD

A famous literary voice once said, "I took the road less traveled by, and that has made all the difference". What was not considered is that all the roads, paths, journeys and dreams, end in the same place. The more solitary, less traveled paths may miss the wealth of human experiences that are often the most memorable parts of our lives. Interacting with others about their journeys, sharing stories, and enjoying the richness of love, friendship, and laughter is really what brings joy and makes all the difference. The journey ends far too quickly and the most frequent regrets at the end are not having spent enough time with loved ones and not taking the time to be happier. So, share the road. Sing out loud. Dance. Love many. Eat cake. Laugh, and celebrate life to the fullest with those you meet along the trodden road.

ART ATRIBUTION

Poem	Attribution	Notes
Cover	Frankie McCarthy	Local Artist in Vienna, VA
Title	Cottonbro	pexels-cottonbro-4911170
Copyright pg	Miguel Padriñán	pexels-miguel-á-padriñán-19670
Dedication	Many	Ten different Pexels photographs
Table Contents	Miguel Padrinan	pexels-miguel-á-padriñán-194098
Dedication pg 1	Madison Inouye	pexels-madison-inouye-1831234
Dedication pg 2	E. Grossgasteiger	pexels-eberhard-grossgasteiger
Forward	Frank Cone	pexels-photo-3573556
This Is	Deeana Arts	pexels-deeana-arts-1646981 (1)
Profit Prophet	Pixabay	pexels-pixabay-106152
Tom Yesterday	Anthony	pexels-anthony-132428
Candlelight	Tucă Bianca	pexels-tucă-bianca-360177
The King	Gavin Seim	pexels-gavin-seim-3259997
Tangle Are We	Salah Özil	pexels-salah-özil-10919385 (1)
New Thought	Ketut Subiyanto	pexels-ketut-subiyanto-4350283
Seclusion	M. Venter	pexels-m-venter-1659437
Nobody	Aynur Latfullin	pexels-aynur-latfullin-11173168
Ocean & Coast	Daniel Jurin	pexels-photo-1835712
Our Country	Frankie McCarthy	Local Artist in Vienna, VA
'Til Death	Bret Jordon	pexels-brett-jordan-11591677
'Til Death short	Rodnae Produc	pexels-rodnae-productions-8865116
We are two I's	Ivan Puglisi	pexels-ivan-puglisi-2642267
Seafarer	Frankie McCarthy	Local Artist in Vienna, VA
Frogs	The Dodo	https://www.thedodo.com/in-the-wild/frog-farm-footage-china

Poem	Attribution	Notes
Secret	meruyert-gonullu	pexels-meruyert-gonullu-6034025
Music Beats War	Pixabay	pexels-pixabay-210766
	Pixabay	pexels-pixabay-164935
Daydream	Johannes Plenio	pexels-johannes-plenio-1125774
Our Song	Mateusz Dach	pexels-mateusz-dach-320335
Calamity	Elianne Dipp	pexels-elianne-dipp-4666754
Godzilla	publicly available	Walmart advertisement for toy
Anger Relinq	P. Shuvrasankha	pexels-shuvrasankha-paul-2610219
Children Dream	Xiong Nicollazzi	pexels-nicollazzi-xiong-668353
Raining	P. Oleksandr	pexels-oleksandr-pidvalnyi-2144326
Frghtmare	Cottonbro	pexels-cottonbro-7181906
Goddess Eyes	Otto Noelle	pexels-noelle-otto-906052
Mirror	Andre Mouton	pexels-andre-mouton-1207875
Altitude Above	Alfonso Dubuc	pexels-alfonso-dubuc-4485651
Monarch	роман-микрюков	pexels-роман-микрюков-8647126
Strummin'	Rodnae Productions	pexels-rodnae-productions-6129685
Awakening	Bloggers Wizard	pexels-bloggerswizard-5384729
Afterword	Pixabay	pexels-pixabay-276299
	R. Tsukata	pexels-ryutaro-tsukata-5220100
	E.C. Lopez	pexels-enric-cruz-lópez-6272213
	J. Hayaku	pexels-hayaku-julie-8592941
End Page	W. Moretti	pexels-wendel-moretti-1925630
	J. Borba	pexels-jonathan-borba-2873058
Attribution	Pixabay	pexels-pixabay-220182
Author Bio	Pixabay	pexels-pixabay-326333

AUTHOR BIO

Poet, humorist, and children's book author Remo Perini first published some of the poems found in this book with the National Library of Poetry. His prolific writing has spanned decades which resulted in this debut book of poetry, *Evens and Beginnings, A Collection of Odds and Ends*. Remo's unique poetic artistry has been influenced by many progressive artists including musician Lori Anderson and writing techniques used by such greats as Kurt Vonnegut. Some works are designed to draw the reader in by playfully offering tidbits of meaning, while obscuring depth of understanding using words that may be vaguely familiar but have been artistically molded.

Creative ideas such as *Evens and Beginnings, A Collection of Odds and Ends*, come from his lifetime of thoughtful observation and broad experience while some of his humorous offerings are fictional or based on warping historic facts. Remo believes that a great book is not dictated by its subject but by the skill of the writer: "A great writer can write about a speck of dust that has been laying on a shelf for ten years and make it interesting and intriguing," says Remo. His hope is that all of his readers come away from his books with a sense of joy, curiosity, and/or humor from their experience.

Remo grew up in NY the eldest son of two elementary school teachers. Moving to San Jose, CA after college graduation, he hosted a radio show on 89.7FM KFJC, called The *Gateway to Infinity,* and attained local celebrity through his satirical feature, "Bay Area Laundromats". Responding to a press release, David Letterman's producer said "We love your Laundromat idea but we only bring on guests of national interest." Then, displaying the sincerest form of flattery, Letterman aired a laundromat segment the next week.

In addition to his 2022 debut book *Evens and Beginnings*, his second book of poetry, *Strumming on the Old* Banjo will be released in 2023 (or maybe 2024) and he has four upcoming books in other genres: his book of humor, *HA!* (late 2022), and a series of three children's books with a protagonist named Eustace, beginning with *Eustace and the Christmas Swim*. These will be out sequentially in 2023, 2024, and 2025, illustrated by a well-known caricature artist, Danny O'Leary. The 2022 books of humor and of poetry are each dedicated to his father and mother, respectively. Remo lives with two sons, Nico and Mateo and a poodle named Enzo in Vienna, VA, just West of DC. Remo aspires to become the Bard of Vienna, or the Bard of anyplace looking for a Bard. Please contact Remo if you need a Bard.